True Ghos..

REAL HAUNTED HOSPITALS AND MENTAL ASYLUMS

BY ZACHERY KNOWLES

Real Haunted Hospitals and Mental Asylums Copyright © 2015 by Zachery Knowles.

All rights reserved. No part of this book may be reproduced in any form without permission in writing from the author. Reviewers may quote brief passages in reviews

ISBN: 1517759757

ISBN-13: 978-1517759759

Disclaimer

No part of this publication may be reproduced or transmitted in any form or by any means, mechanical or electronic, including photocopying or recording, or by any information storage and retrieval system, or transmitted by email without permission in writing from the publisher.

While all attempts have been made to verify the information provided in this publication, neither the author nor the publisher assumes any responsibility for errors, omissions, or contrary interpretations of the subject matter herein.

This book is for entertainment purposes only. The views expressed are those of the author alone, and should not be taken as expert instruction or commands. The reader is responsible for his or her own actions.

Adherence to all applicable laws and regulations, including international, federal, state, and local governing professional licensing, business practices, advertising, and all other aspects of doing business in the US, Canada, or any other jurisdiction is the sole responsibility of the purchaser or reader.

Neither the author nor the publisher assumes any responsibility or liability whatsoever on the behalf of the purchaser or reader of these materials.

Any perceived slight of any individual or organization is purely unintentional.

YOUR FREE GIFT

As a way of saying thanks for your purchase, I'm offering a free eBook to readers of my *True Ghost Stories* series.

To instantly download the PDF version of my book, *Real Black-Eyed Kids*, all you need to do is visit:

www.realhorror.net

CONTENTS

INTRODUCTION 7
    WAVERLY HILLS SANITORIUM 12
    TAUNTON STATE HOSPITAL 19
    OLD CHANGI HOSPITAL 25
    BEECHWORTH LUNATIC ASYLUM......................30
    ROYAL HOPE HOSPITAL 37
    METROPOLITAN STATE HOSPITAL.....................42
    PRIPYAT HOSPITAL 48
    KUHN MEMORIAL STATE HOSPITAL 53
    THE OLD MENTAL HOSPITAL 57
    TRANS-ALLEGHENY LUNATIC ASYLUM 61
    BEELITZ-HEILSTÄTTEN 66
    WOLFE MANOR..71
    WHITTINGHAM MENTAL HOSPITAL 76

SLEEP WELL..83

INTRODUCTION

For people who believe in the paranormal—ghosts, spirits, and other unexplainable encounters—most will agree that old hospitals are the most haunted places you can visit. Even those who don't want to believe in the supernatural have no choice but to agree with them after exploring an abandoned hospital themselves.

I've always had an interest in witnessing—if not understanding—the things on earth that are outside of our realm of understanding. Who were these ghosts and spirits and why do they linger? What do they hope to accomplish by haunting certain areas? Do they even have a choice?

Recently I started to wonder why old hospitals are such hotspots for paranormal activity. My first thought was an obvious one—a lot of people died there. But a lot of people died at the medical center down the road from my house, and no one's mentioned seeing any apparitions or phantoms there.

Once I started digging into the histories of these old hospitals, sanitariums, and asylums, I discovered the real reasons why they are often so frighteningly haunted: life at these institutions was so dark, so bleak, and so helpless that no hospital could possibly exist by those standards today.

Before the days of penicillin and common vaccines, hospitals were more like quarantine zones than places of healing. Called sanitariums, hospitals were built to keep diseased people away from everyone else. Other than receiving a few primitive and disturbing surgeries, patients were often expected just to die. So die they did, trapped, after suffering miserably at the hospital from an easily curable disease by today's standards.

Children were often among the sick, either as patients or because their parents were dying, and there was nowhere else for them to go. Today, the spirits of those children linger, playing in the rooms and singing through the halls.

But it's not all fun and games.

The cruelty of a life cut short can lead to the most disturbing apparitions. Take Mary, for instance, the little girl who "wasn't normal." Left behind at Waverly Hills Sanatorium, Mary went from young and innocent in life to something horrific in death. Her ghost has become the stuff of nightmares. And she's not even the scariest part of Waverly—that would be the infamous Room 502. But you'll have to read on to learn what horrors lie within that disturbing room.

And then there were the hospitals caught in the crosshairs of the world's deadliest wars. In the days where the body count was thought to relate directly to who was winning a war, hospitals were strategic facilities to hold, no matter which side you were on. Ironically, despite their original purpose, many wartime hospitals ended up acting as both a prison and execution center. These hospitals are home to the most threatening spirits. Based on the stories, it would seem that they're on a mission to ensure that the horrors and atrocities they experienced will never be erased from our memories.

Take Old Changi for example, a military hospital in Singapore during World War II. Trespassers at this historical site have time and again been struck by a temporary madness, claiming they stumbled upon the scene of a gory bloodbath—the mass execution of Japanese soldiers. The temporary—and vividly accurate—vision burns a permanent, disturbing memory into visitors' minds, making them think twice about trespassing again.

Then finally there are the asylums—in my opinion the most disturbing of the lot. Before therapeutic drug treatments were available, back when mental illness was hardly understood, the only way to control abnormal behavior was by force. Rather than managing their illness at home with their families, the mentally ill were locked up by the thousands, in mega facilities designed to work like prisons. The only difference was that prison inmates weren't subjected to the cruel and painful 'treatments' that mental patients were.

While it was easy to check into a lunatic asylum, checking out was almost impossible. So many patients lived and died there, only to live again as spirits trapped in the building that claimed their lives. Witnessing an apparition is one thing, but encountering a mentally insane one is quite another.

Whether staff or patients, mental institutions house a disturbing cast of characters. Case in point, Taunton State Hospital. This Massachusetts asylum was the long-term home to Jolly Jane, a former nurse and serial killer, it's estimated she killed 31 of her patients. I suppose it's patients like Jane that made people feel relieved that asylums were under such a strong lock and key.

As time went on, doctors became better at their craft. They cured the incurable diseases and found better ways to help the thousands of mentally ill that filled every city. Sanatoriums and asylums lost their purpose, and one-by-one were abandoned. War tactics and technologies have changed since the 1940s, leading to less use of wartime hospitals. But the buildings themselves have historic value, and many of them are still standing today. What remains within them is even more disturbing than the dark histories themselves.

As my increasing obsession with old hospitals from a different era grew, I started compiling a list of some of the most intriguing, most spooky, and most disturbing abandoned hospitals around the world. I've devoted a chapter to each, detailing their dark histories and speculating on how they led to the hauntings of today. Each chapter also describes the details of the most common ghostly encounters. Whether or not these sightings are based on myth or true horrors—I leave that for the reader to decide.

WAVERLY HILLS SANITORIUM

In the early 1900s America, the country was ravaged by tuberculosis (TB), a deadly and incurable disease. The bacterial infection causes painful growths in the lungs that make it increasingly difficult to breathe, resulting in a slow and difficult death. Called the White Plague, the highly contagious disease can overcome entire families and, in some cases, entire towns. Something, anything, needed to be done to contain it, and fast.

Fast-forward to 1910, when Waverly Hills Sanatorium was established on a high hill in Jefferson County, Kentucky. A hospital for the treatment of TB patients, doctors and nurses did their best to keep it as self-sufficient as possible to limit the risk of infection spreading to the surrounding community. They maintained their own essential services, and hospital workers weren't allowed to transfer for fear of spreading the disease.

As soon as Waverly Hills opens, it was overrun with sick patients. The hospital was rebuilt and expanded to meet demand, including the addition of a children's pavilion. This ward was designed to house children with TB, as well as the children of sick patients who had no one else to care for them.

Diagnosis of TB often meant death. This was long before the days of antibiotics. Doctors were at a loss on how to treat the disease. Fresh air, rest, and proper nutrition were thought to be the best treatments. Especially fresh air. It was so important that patients were often placed on open patios or in front of open windows—regardless of the weather. Fresh air was more important than staying out of the snow.

As the illness progressed, more desperate measures were required. Exposing a patient's lungs to ultraviolet light in a so-called sunroom was one common treatment. An alternative method involved placing balloons into a patient's lungs and inflating them to encourage the lungs to breathe. Then there was the Last Resort, as the doctors called it, surgically removing some ribs and the surrounding muscle tissue to ease the pressure on the lungs. Patients rarely survived it.

For cases such as these, nurses had the Death Tunnel—a 500-foot chute used to lower dead bodies out of the hospital and to the bottom of the hill. It wasn't just used for convenience; it helped protect the other patients' mental health. The sight of so many bodies leaving through the front door would have been devastating for patient morale.

It was business as usual at Waverly Hills until it closed in 1961. New antibiotic treatments managed to do what UV exposure and removing body parts could not, and TB was almost completely eradicated.

Unfortunately for the patients of Waverly Hills, many of them entered the hospital by the front door and left via the Death Tunnel. Keeping up with the disease left most records in disorder, so no one knows exactly how many people died within Waverly Hills' walls. Speculators say 63,000, though historians opt for a more modest 8,212 deaths.

After the TB hospital had closed, Waverly Hills was reopened as Woodhaven Geriatric Center. No one paid too much attention to what went on at the facility after that, but maybe they should have. In 1982, Woodhaven was closed by the state because of patient neglect. For 20 years, Waverly Hills lay vacant.

Well, almost. Despite its disuse, crumbing walls, and increasingly decrepit state, the homeless flocked to Waverly Hills for a dry place to sleep. It also became a favorite haunt of vandals and partiers looking for a thrill. That's when the stories started.

The paranormal sightings at Waverly Hills began as whispers in the Jefferson County community. Mysterious doors slamming, lights on when there was no power to the building, the sounds of footsteps in empty rooms, disembodied voices.

No one paid the ramblings of hoodlums and the homeless much mind, but the stories became so frequent, they could no longer be ignored. They even piqued the interest of the Louisville Ghost Hunters Society, who came to investigate the hospital and bring its secrets into the light. Since then, the sanatorium has been dubbed one of the most haunted places in the world.

Maybe that's because you don't even have to venture inside the building to spot something eerie. Countless people have seen the same desperate, spectral woman running out the front entrance of Waverly Hills. Witnesses saw her hands and legs bound in chains—blood dripping from her wrists and ankles. She screams desperately for someone to help her, then disappears into thin air. Could she have been one of the many victims of TB who died at the hospital? Or one of the tortured residents of the prison-like elderly home that followed? No one can say.

One thing's for sure; the wailing woman isn't alone. The spectral appearances of countless children, likely young victims of TB, still roam the hospital. Many visitors have heard the sounds of children laughing and playing on the building's roof, even singing nursery rhymes like "Ring Around the Rosie." When visitors investigated the strange sounds, no one was to be found. It makes sense that the spirits of children might linger on the roof—they were often taken up there for heliotherapy, where doctors exposed them to the sun and fresh air in hopes of alleviating TB symptoms.

More sinister children can be found deeper in the building. On the third floor, the ghost of a little girl has been seen so many times that visitors have given her a name: Mary. Mary appears in different ways to different people—maybe depending on her mood. Sometimes visitors find her harmlessly—though eerily—playing in the hall with a ball. Sometimes, she's just lurking and watching.

The account of one terrified visitor shows a different side of Mary. The person found a more disturbing Mary in one of the rooms on the third floor and claimed after that Mary "wasn't normal." The little girl appeared to have no eyes—just black gaping sockets where they once were. Witnesses report that the visitor ran screaming from the building and refused to return. Many believe her story, since other witnesses have also reported seeing the same girl peering down at them from windows on the third floor.

Mary's not the only little one roaming Waverly Hills' upper levels. Just one floor up lurks the ghost of Timmy. He's been seen and discussed so much over the years that it's hard to parcel out fact from fiction, but legend has it that he was seven years old when he died at Waverly from TB. And he's been there ever since. Like Mary, Timmy has also been seen playing with a ball in the hallways, but has become more famous for it, since it's the only thing he ever seems to want to do.

Visitors often bring balls with them to the fourth floor in an attempt to communicate with him. Sometimes, the balls seem to move on their own accord. Other times, you can hear a ball bouncing and the sound of a boy's laughter. Several photos taken on the fourth floor have appeared on the Internet showing the eerie face of a young boy peering around the corner. Dying at such a young age, Timmy will forever be a child—one who just wants to play, even if he can't manage to depart the hospital where he languished and passed away.

A few ghostly children might seem harmless enough, but the fifth floor never fails to horrify. The floor looks normal enough, with a couple of nurse's stations and patient rooms. Legend has it that the fifth floor is where the doctors housed the TB patients who had gone mad from their suffering, though no one can say for sure. Reports of strange shapes, disembodied voices, and unexplained sounds are more common on this floor than any other.

Hands down the most mysterious and ghostly part of the floor, possibly even the building, is Room 502. Even just approaching it, visitors often feel incredibly uncomfortable—overwhelmed with a sense of despair. That would make sense, considering the sad history the room holds. Legend has it that in 1928, a nurse was found in the room, hung by the neck from a light fixture. Suicide. The woman had become pregnant out of wedlock by one of the doctors or superintendents of the hospital (no one knows which). Depression overtook her, and rather than admit the shame of being pregnant and not married, she took her own life—and that of her unborn child.

But that wasn't the end of despair for Room 502. In 1932, another nurse jumped out of the window, plunging to her death. Unlike the previous woman, no one knows why this nurse would have taken her own life. People at the time speculated that she may have been pushed out. No one was ever able to solve the mystery.

It would seem that one or both of the nurses who lost their lives in Room 502 still linger today. Some have witnessed the complete apparition of a woman in white lingering in the doorway of Room 502. Others have seen strange shadows and heard whispers. One thing's for sure; Room 502 is not a welcoming place. Often, the door closes on its own accord. Many have heard a clear and firm voice saying, "Get out." Visitors can't help but wonder if that's what the nurse heard before she was pushed out the window.

Nowadays, it's not possible to wander through Waverly Hills on your own, you have to go on a guided tour. With Waverly's long history of disease, suffering, patient neglect, and untimely deaths, the residents never stop trying to make their story heard by those who listen closely enough. Recently, the hospital was purchased by a private couple, who plan to convert it into a four-star hotel for ghost-lovers and thrill-seekers. Now the big question is: will the nurses allow anyone staying in Room 502 to last the night?

TAUNTON STATE HOSPITAL

In 1854, Massachusetts's Taunton State Hospital opened. Commissioned by the government because of overcrowding in the state's existing mental hospitals, the new building was coined the *State Lunatic Hospital at Taunton*.

The hospital was impressively massive, designed to separate patients based on sex and severity of illness. It was built on a hilltop to give patients access to the only real treatments for insanity at the time: fresh air and quiet scenery.

Within the first eight weeks of opening, Taunton received 250 patients. By 1873, more than 500 people lived there. The demand for places to house the insane grew greater, and soon Taunton was expanded to include group homes, crisis centers, sick wards, and juvenile housing. Young delinquents with a history of violent behavior or mental health issues were sent to Taunton by the state.

Often, patients who were committed and subject to 'treatment' were not actually mentally ill. Taunton, in particular, became known by historians as a place to lock up troublesome immigrants, especially the Irish. Most who came to Taunton never left. Soon, it resembled a self-contained city.

As such a large and well-equipped facility, Taunton was home to many high-profile patients. Probably the sickest among them was Jane Toppan, nicknamed *Jolly Jane*.

A former nurse, Jolly Jane was also a confessed serial killer. One of her favorite pastimes was administering lethal doses of drugs to her helpless patients, and lying next to them while they slowly drifted into death. Thirty-one people lost their lives at Jolly Jane's hand, at least that she admitted to. When put on trial, she managed to convince the jury that she was insane, sending her to Taunton for the rest of her life. She was once said to have admitted that her life's desire was to kill more people, specifically helpless people, than any man or woman who ever lived.

On the surface, the lunatic hospital's deranged patients might seem like the most frightening thing about the place, but the nocturnal activities of the staff are what really gave Taunton its horrific reputation.

Standard practice at many mental hospitals of the time was to try experimental treatments, including water and shock therapy. Water therapy involved placing patients in scalding and freezing baths of water, to see what effect it had on the body. How this was supposed to improve the sanity of patients, no one really knows.

While you can't blame doctors for using what they thought were the best practices of the day, heavy and persistent rumors circulated about the "extracurricular" activities of workers at Taunton.

Some say that hospital workers would take the most incapacitated patients down to the basement to perform cult rituals that involved torture and even sacrifices to Satan. For some doctors, Taunton may have been an opportunity to perform experiments that wouldn't have been possible elsewhere. Rumors fly that patients' limbs were removed and reattached to other patients to see how well the body reacted. Usually, these experiments resulted in death.

It all may sound a little far-fetched, but the mysterious Satanic symbols found throughout the basement of the hospital can't be explained any other way. Even more convincing is the legacy the basement has held ever since those dark days. Many staff without knowledge of the basement's dark past reported feelings of discomfort and despair whenever they entered it, as well as unexplained cold spots that seemed to follow them through the room.

Even many hardened criminals, residents at Taunton, who were already accustomed to dank rooms and dark cells refused to enter the basement to do chores, often losing privileges because of it. Whatever punishments they were threatened with were not enough to convince them to spend more than a few minutes in the hellish basement.

One staff member couldn't blame them. He only made it to the bottom step of the stairs before he felt forced to stop. He closed his eyes and saw flashes of what he believed were the horrific events that transpired there over the years. He quit his job, left the hospital, and never came back. To this day, he can't bear to explain what he saw.

Almost as well-known as the infamous basement at Taunton are the surrounding woods. Legend has it that many members of the town—not just the hospital staff—performed bizarre cult rituals there. Back in the day, people reported hearing moaning, screaming, and loud bangs coming from the Taunton Woods. The really strange thing is that people today still hear them. Some say the sounds are all that remain of the tortured souls who were brutally sacrificed there.

Parts of Taunton were still in-use until recent years, and one patient, in particular, had a very frightening experience in the woods. Hoping for freedom, he escaped the main facility and disappeared into a cemetery located in the woods. Deciding to lay low and hash out a plan to escape the area unseen, the man spent the night in the cemetery.

In the dark that night, he felt cold hands touch his shoulder and realized that he had been caught. But when he raised his arms and turned around, he saw no captor. Instead, an almost indiscernible voice whisper in his ear, "Leave." So that's what he did. Breathlessly, he headed back to Taunton Hospital and turned himself in.

The basement and woods are the most unsettling parts of Taunton, full of tortured, lost souls. It would seem, however, that the lingering spirits haunt beyond those areas.

A large number of patients reported seeing the apparition of a man lurking in their rooms in the main building. Sometimes, he appears as no more than a shadow, but somehow manages to crawl across the wall. Other times, he's nearly solid, but looks freakishly tall, as if stretched out. However, there are a few things about his appearance that are always consistent: he's male, always appears in the corner of the room, and no patient has ever been able to see his face.

Other strange occurrences in the hospital are less apparent, though no less unsettling. A large number of staff members working in the Goss Building claim to have seen a man wearing white, wandering the halls of the third floor. Others claimed that the lights in their room would turn on or off on their own, or complain of strange, unexplained noises from vacant areas of the hospital.

While the main ward of Taunton State Hospital was shut down in 1975, the hospital remained in use in some capacity until an unexplained fire partially burned it down in 2008. Its long-term use made ghostly sightings a regular problem—frightening residents and workers alike. Despite efforts in Massachusetts to repair and restore the building after the fire, it was demolished in 2009. One would hope this was enough to put some of the tortured souls of Taunton to rest. But then again, the stories coming from the woods and cemetery continue.

OLD CHANGI HOSPITAL

Built while death and destruction were rife, war hospitals always seem to carry the most gruesome histories. Case in point: Old Changi Hospital. Originally called the Royal Air Force Hospital, Old Changi was built by the British in 1935 to care for colonial and local troops in Singapore. That might have been it for the tale of Old Changi, but with conflict comes war, and with war comes conquest.

In 1942, the Japanese attacked Singapore, taking control of the country and hospital. Suddenly, what was once a place to care for the British soldiers and their allies, became a prison camp where many met their deaths.

Old Changi became a repository to store the British, Australian, Indian, and Malaysian soldiers, as well as any troublesome Singaporeans with anti-Japanese sentiments. The hospital-turned-prison-camp was run by the

Kempeitai, the Japanese secret police, known worldwide for their brutal tactics. Prisoners of war were regularly submitted to torture of the cruelest and most unusual varieties. One Australian soldier recounted his interrogation:

"The interviewer produced a small piece of wood like a meat skewer, pushed that into my left ear, and tapped it with a small hammer. I think I fainted some time after it went through the drum. I remember the last excruciating sort of pain, and I must have gone out for some time because I was revived with a bucket of water. Eventually it healed but of course I couldn't hear with it. I have never been able to hear since."

The Japanese used scare tactics on those they allowed to live. They placed iron stakes outside of the YMCA and Cathay Buildings of Old Changi. They then displayed the severed hands of executed prisoners on the stakes for all to see.

Thousands of people died at the hospital before the Japanese lost and the war ended. As the hospital changed hands back to the British, many of the Japanese soldiers were executed there in turn. Old Changi, which was supposed to be a place of healing, witnessed a lot of death on both sides.

In 1975, the British withdrew from Singapore, and the hospital truly returned to its original purpose, serving the sick and wounded from Singapore's army as well as the general public. Old Changi was finally abandoned in the 1990s as newer facilities were built.

While Old Changi's violent history is well documented, the public has also come forward with stories of abnormal and unexplainable occurrences at the abandoned hospital—by the thousands. It is considered the most haunted place in Singapore, and the locals confirm it by fervently warning visitors to stay away from the area at night.

Those brave—foolish?—enough to visit commonly claim to have seen apparitions or shadows of people, hear disembodied screams, witnessed strange, erratic lights, and scented phantom scents.

Some claim to see a small boy throughout the hospital, always found sitting and staring into nothingness. The boy looks sad, and those who see him feel a strong sense of the emotion even after leaving the building. The most horrific stories come from the numerous people who reported stumbling across a gory bloodbath—the mass execution of Japanese soldiers.

As the stories of strange sights and sounds at Old Changi continue to pour in, the hospital has become a regular attraction for teenagers and thrill seekers. Singaporean native Andreas Chan was once one such teenager—she visited Old Changi with her friends quite a few times when she was young. Most of their visits consisted of the usual thrills—dank, dark rooms and strange smells that piqued their curiosity more than their fears. But what happened on one visit had them leaving the hospital with chills down their spines.

Two of the four girls were exploring the second floor when they heard a loud bang on the ceiling of the first floor. They ran over to the source of the sound and stomped their feet on the floor, thinking their friends had been banging on the ceiling to scare them. They heard another loud bang in return. After, they ran downstairs to confront their friends and found the first floor empty. What's more, the ceiling was so high, it would have been impossible for anyone to bang on it without a ladder.

Chan and her friend later found their other friends on the second floor. They had been exploring another room and had no idea what sounds the other girls were talking about. Events took a turn for the scarier when one of the girls mentioned hearing a voice complaining that they were making too much noise, even though there was no one else in the building but the four of them. The voice had offered this warning in Hokkien, the main Chinese dialect spoken in Singapore when the hospital first opened.

Andreas Chan's account is just one of the thousands of strange and unusual happenings at Old Changi. The notion that the hospital was haunted became so popular that a crew produced a mockumentary film on the premises, called *Haunted Changi*.

The film was released in 2010, and while it was meant to be a bit humorous, the real ghosts of Changi weren't laughing. The crew was in for some real paranormal activity that they hadn't bargained for. Many complained of hearing loud bangs from empty parts of the hospital, disembodied voices, and groping of unseen hands. Several reported seeing the apparition of a woman with what appeared to be a black aura. The most ironic—and disturbing—part about it was that they also managed to catch a shadow person on video while filming the movie. They decided to leave the video of the lurking figure in the final cut of the film, lending some unintended credibility to the message of *Haunted Changi*.

After garnering so much spooky and unexpected interest, many attempts have been made to plan a reconstruction of the dead and decaying hospital. All have fallen through for one reason or another, and the historic building lies vacant to this day.

To some, it's a paranormal haven, sure to leave visitors with chills down their spines and sights they can't unsee. For others, the building is a monument of war and perseverance. No matter which camp you're in, Old Changi (and maybe its ghosts) is a testament to a particularly gruesome and unforgiving time in human history.

BEECHWORTH LUNATIC ASYLUM

By the late 1860s in Australia, Victoria's only mental institution was bursting at the seams with mentally ill patients. In response, the Mayday Hills Lunatic Asylum was opened to house and "treat" up to 1,200 patients. Getting admitted was a simple affair, requiring only two signatures from friends or relatives who wanted you locked up. Getting out was much more difficult.

Later renamed the Beechworth Lunatic Asylum, Mayday Hills was open for 128 years and brings with it a history of strange medical practices and care. The first superintendent himself may have been a bit off—he believed that the moon caused insanity and refused to go outside at nighttime without an umbrella.

Housing a mixture of 600 men and 600 women, the Beechworth Lunatic Asylum was almost always full, though whether the patients deserved to be there is a different story.

Many of the patents were not actually clinically insane. In order to leave the hospital, a patient would need eight signatures certifying that they were fit for the outside world. Most of the doctors, nurses, and caretakers at Beechworth viewed their patients as liabilities beyond cure, and lacked the care and compassion of today's caregivers. As a result, many completely sane people spent their lives locked in Beechworth's expansive wards.

While freedom might have been a futile endeavor, access to the latest treatments for insanity were in abundance. Beechworth was equipped with the latest tools for handling and treating the insane. Doctors had access to a fully-equipped lab for operations, autopsies, and any other experiments they might like to try. The shelves of the lab were said to be filled with jars of body parts from unlucky patients, though after a fire had damaged the ward, the jars were removed.

Before the 1950s, psychiatric medication was unavailable, so shackles and straitjackets were often used to help control patients' aggressive and unruly behavior. The Grevillia Wing of the hospital was home to the electro-shock treatment facility, an incredibly routine treatment for the clinically insane. No one would dream of treating a patient with electro-shock therapy today—the shocks were strong, and often forced the patients' bodies to contract into unnatural positions, snapping bones, ligaments, and teeth in the process.

For good reason, the Grevillia Wing was the part of the hospital that all patients feared most, and stories still circulate about mass treatments where almost everyone in the hospital was shocked in group sessions. If they weren't insane before, they certainly were afterwards.

No one seems to know exactly how many patients died in the Beechworth Lunatic Asylum, though it's estimated to be between 3,000 and 9,000. Most left this world as victims of their illness; wasting away, taking their own lives, or suffering the effects of aggressive "treatments." The less troubled and more docile patients died of old age, though a few deaths were a lot more suspicious.

An example of this was the death of a nameless Jewish woman, committed to the women's wing of Beechworth. She kept to herself mostly and didn't cause any trouble as long as she had her cigarettes. People would most often find her sitting in a high-story window, smoking. One day, another patient wanted to have some of her cigarettes. Maybe they asked politely at first—no one could say. But the woman was never one for sharing, and wouldn't give any up. One thing led to another, and suddenly the Jewish woman found herself tumbling out the window to her death.

No one knows what ultimately became of the other patient, but everyone remembers what happened to the Jewish woman. They left her body lying in the grass for two days before moving her. You see, in Jewish tradition, no one is allowed to touch the deceased until a Rabbi has seen the body. Since the closest Rabbi had to come all the way from Melbourne, the woman's gruesome end was a sight for all to see for more than 48 hours.

It's possible the woman didn't appreciate such a steadfast observance of her religious beliefs. In more recent years, many have reported seeing the eerie outline of a woman lurking where her body fell so many years before. Others claim to have seen a woman's face in the window where she loved to sit and smoke.

Escaping from Beechworth was nearly impossible, though that didn't stop people from trying. The most unruly patients were locked in cells, while the others were kept on the grounds by twistedly-named Ha-Ha Walls—high trenched walls that no patient could ever hope to climb. Despite these securities, one man disappeared from the compound long ago. The asylum staff and surrounding community searched desperately to find him—no one wanted a committed lunatic roaming the streets. Eventually, they had to give him up as lost.

Then, several weeks after they abandoned the search, someone found the asylum's pet dog, Max, happily gnawing on a meaty bone. On closer inspection, Max's snack was the remains of a human leg. The asylum staff conducted another search by the gate house where the leg was found. A suspicious looking shadow and horrific smell helped the searchers uncover the patient's body—in a tree. His body had managed to decompose so much that his leg had fallen to the ground for Max to find.

No one ever discovered how the patient actually died in the tree, but many since claim to have seen the man's ghost lurking near the asylum's entrance. He never did get out.

An active asylum for 128 years, Beechworth was witness to a lot of pain and suffering by patients before it was decommissioned in 1995. Now, it has been partially converted into a satellite campus for La Trobe University, a hotel, and a tour facility. However many parts, including the Grevillia wing (home to the electro-shock facility), have been left unused and dilapidated. Since most of the asylum has been transformed and is now full of guests, paranormal sightings are everywhere.

Matron Sharpe was once a caretaker at the Asylum, and has been spotted by so many witnesses that she can't be ignored. In life, she was known for her compassionate care of patients, which was uncharacteristic in her time. In death, she seems to be carrying on her routine. Matron Sharpe is most often seen with patients in the Grevillia wing, comforting them before electro-shock therapy. Those who spot her often feel calm and comforted, despite the overwhelming chill that fills the room. That said, it's probably easier for Matron Sharpe to comfort a person who's just seen a ghost than a patient who's about to get the shock of his life.

The Asylum's Recreation Hall was one of the few places where patients could relax, perform plays and concerts, and attend Sunday Mass. In 1939, it was converted into a cinema for inmates. As one of the few places that regularly brought joy to the lives of prisoners, it makes sense that they would visit the Recreation Hall in death.

What doesn't make any sense is that the most commonly-sighted specter in the wing is a desperate-looking young girl who approaches people and tries to talk to them. Others have seen the ghost of an elderly man gazing longingly out of the window in the Bell Tower. Clearly, Beechworth's history holds a lot more than meets the eye, as some of the former inmates are trying to communicate.

Even more disturbing is that despite the fact that the asylum was only for adults, numerous workers at Beechworth have heard the distinct sounds of children laughing throughout the hospital, but were never able to track down where the voices were coming from. Others claim to have felt someone pulling on their clothes and poking them in the ribs in the Bijou theatre. What secrets does this asylum hold that children would choose to linger in such a place? Or maybe they can't leave.

Tours of the hospital never fail to spook someone—guests often describe seeing a serious-looking man following them through the halls. Behind the man, two other strange figures follow, joking and laughing. Some say the serious man is a former doctor. That makes sense with his stern attitude—he could be one of the therapists, pondering his next experimental treatment on his way to the laboratory. But the identities of the laughing men following him remain a mystery.

Guests of the hotel also frequently report hearing footsteps in the hallway that belong to no one, and tapping on the old glass windows. Beechworth is a haunting ground for doctors, patients, and workers alike.

Not spooked enough? The Beechworth Ghost Tour is the most popular in mainland Australia. Go and see for yourself.

ROYAL HOPE HOSPITAL

St. Augustine, Florida is the oldest permanent European settlement in the United States. With it comes a long history filled with the struggle and suffering of a developing nation. Many wars left scars on early America, especially in the south. One hospital, called Royal Hope, witnessed some of the worst of it.

Originally called Our Lady of Guadalupe, Royal Hope was first opened in St. Augustine as a Spanish military hospital, where it treated the sick and wounded from 1784-1821. It burned down but was soon replaced by an exact replica to house the wounded of the Seminole War. Historians say that at least 70% of the men who came to Royal Hope survived the hospital, but given how long it was in operation, thousands found their final resting place there.

Today, Royal Hope serves as a Spanish Military Hospital Museum, where visitors can learn more about the war and how the soldiers were treated before modern medicine. However, a discovery by St. Augustine Public Works has left people wondering what was actually going on at Royal Hope all those years ago. Everyone knew that Royal Hope once kept a cemetery where soldiers could receive a proper Catholic burial after succumbing to their wounds. But a few years ago, workers were digging to repair plumbing near the hospital and were surprised to uncover piles and piles of human bones.

Most people figured that the historians underestimated just how big this cemetery was. However, the bones themselves suggest a different story. Why were so many bones piled together, without any markers or organization? The discovery appeared much unlike a traditional Catholic burial, leaving locals to scratch their heads over what happened to all these people, and wonder why their burial was kept a secret.

Rumors began to fly that the hospital had been built on an ancient Timucuan Indian burial site, a likely idea considering the area. No one was ever able to confirm this one way or another, as the bones were quickly reburied where they were found, out of respect for the dead.

Even if the bones can't speak, the ghosts of Royal Hope sure seem to. As an active museum for the war, people regularly sight strange and unexplainable things that suggest the hospital has its own story to tell. Many visitors to the sick ward have witnessed old beds and furniture moving across the room on their own—

sometimes bumping into their legs, as if trying to draw their attention to something.

Two tourists, in particular, spotted what they could only describe as a phantom. They claim that it appeared in front of them only long enough to look at their faces before vanishing. Could it have been the spirit of a lost soldier? No one can say. Though others have reported strange sightings that suggest that, at least in Royal Hope, the Seminole War still rages on.

Many have heard the distinct sound of marching footsteps coming from the upper floor of the hospital that has been vacant for decades. Anyone who went upstairs to investigate the sounds discovered nothing. More have noticed the distinct and alarming smell of sulfur, as if from gun smoke, which improbably lingers after all these years.

Other visitors to the hospital learned more than they bargained for about the despair and suffering that once permeated the building during its long history. Groans and shouts are often heard coming from otherwise empty rooms. The Prayer Room is particularly well known for these unexplainable noises. As the place where dying soldiers would have received their last rights, it was often a place of ultimate despair.

Visitors can still feel it—describing strange feelings of loss and helplessness when entering the room. People often hear pained groans coming from the Prayer Room, accompanied by the hushed prayers of whoever guided the soldier into the afterlife.

Passing away to the sound of soothing prayer may have been the highlight for many soldiers at Royal Hope. The strangled cries of one man can often be heard coming from the old apothecary, where workers administered pharmaceuticals to the sick. People who visit the room have reported seeing distinct shadows moving back and forth as if lost, confused, or trapped. Could they be tortured souls from a disturbed ancient burial ground, unable to find peace in death? Many wonder.

Today, the Surgeon's Office serves as a display room for the outdated and disturbing medical equipment used at the time. The equipment draws a lot of interest, especially because numerous visitors have witnessed it shaking—all on its own. Two different people have also confessed that they felt someone grabbing them and their clothes, refusing to let go until they managed to rip themselves free. Maybe the doctor's still in?

They aren't the only ones who have admitted they were grabbed by some unseen presence. Several others have the scratches to prove it on their stomachs and backs. Some of the scratches even look like they could be attempts at a message—the word 'help.' That might seem a little hard to believe, but the abundance of photo and video recordings of spooky, unexplainable apparitions surface from visitors to the hospital every year.

Between the mysterious piles of bones and history of needless suffering at Royal Hope, it's no wonder people are witnessing so many confusing and disturbing messages from lives long lost. Whether or not you believe everything people say about the hauntings of Royal Hope Hospital, it's clear that someone on the other side has something to say as well.

METROPOLITAN STATE HOSPITAL

When Boston's Metropolitan State Hospital opened in 1927, no one had ever seen a psychiatric institution so expansive before. With an administration building, medical and surgical facility, acute and chronic care buildings, psychiatric hospital for children and adolescents, staff housing, morgue, and power plant, the grounds spanned over three different towns in the sprawling Boston region. It was made large out of necessity, but just two years after opening, the hospital had already exceeded its capacity of just over 1000 patients.

Of course, the hospital had to have its own cemetery, to accommodate such an overcrowded facility. But mental hospitals have a patient limit for a reason, and the deaths at the Met appeared to be frequent enough that workers didn't even bother making proper markers for patient graves. By the end of the hospital's operation, the cemetery ended up with 480 anonymous graves, and many more with no marker at all—bodies sunken beneath the ground, their name and stories lost forever.

Among the missing are likely the bodies of 24 child patients, buried on the grounds in the early 1960s. Insanity in children had remained the most elusive mental illness for doctors at the time. The story goes that they were given a medication—strontium—mixed with their milk, as an attempt to quell their unruly behavior. Instead, they were slowly poisoned to death.

The overcrowding and under-qualified hospital staff at the Met continued to take their toll in later years, though we can't say exactly what Melvin Wilson's motives were when he murdered co-patient Anne Marie Davee. It was 1978, and Davee went missing without a trace. No one knew what to think of it for two months, until staff found a hatchet and pieces of Davee's clothing with Wilson. Even more disturbing—he had been carrying around seven of Davee's teeth.

Because it was pretty clear what had happened, the staff didn't bother to investigate further. It wasn't until state mental health workers filed 19 reports of negligence that the Met let the authorities get involved. Two years after Davee's disappearance, Wilson led investigators to her three graves.

You see, Wilson had chopped her to pieces and buried her in three different places on the hospital grounds. Though after so much time, it was difficult to piece her back together, and rumors still fly that parts of her are still out there, buried in other secret places at the hospital that Wilson didn't bother to tell anyone about. He was later transferred to a more secure facility, and the Met forever wore the new nickname, "The Hospital of the Seven Teeth."

With such a long and sinister past, it's no wonder that patients and staff alike began reporting unexplainable events even when the Met was operational. The most frequent sightings were strange shadows that seemed to pass through the walls and halls, appearing in locked rooms as if they owned the place, then disappearing into the shadows.

Too many times nurses heard what sounded like a patient's desperate screams, only to find no one around—the voice was completely disembodied. Though none of that was as frightening as seeing the figures of long-dead patients appearing in their old rooms. For the workers, it happened frequently enough to make them question their own mental state.

One unique feature of the hospital was the maze of underground tunnels. They were originally designed to help people move throughout the hospital during bad weather, though they weren't used often. The tunnels were lit by only a few light bulbs, placed at a distance throughout the passage.

Many staff reported feeling hands grab at their feet, faces, and backs when they walked through the darker areas of a tunnel, but were never able to see anyone there. The feeling of unseen hands frightened workers frequently enough that the tunnels were eventually repurposed for storage. People avoided them after that, though a company of contractors who later had to work in the tunnels mysteriously quit, refusing to go down again and offering no explanation.

In 1992, the hospital closed for good. At an alarming rate, it became dilapidated—filled with a maze of rotting wards, mildewed plaster, asbestos, collapsed ceilings, and waterlogged tunnels. Even after the hospital shut down, the tunnels were filled will all sorts of beds, chairs, and equipment, left dripping and rotting in the echoing darkness. Most upsetting, the tunnels were left filled with patients' belongings, even children's shoes. No one knew why they would be there. Were patients living down there?

As the hospital became more sinister-looking, residents of the surrounding towns began to take more interest in the strange reports by the staff and patients who used to live there. Despite being barracked off from the public, thrill-seekers frequently began visiting the Hospital of the Seven Teeth. It would seem that the spirits were becoming more vocal than before, now that their home had been abandoned.

Heavy doors would slam for no reason, and disembodied whispers drifted down the hallway. More than one Boston local admitted that at times, they felt as if they were experiencing the actual emotions of some long lost patient. They also developed eerie memories of hospital procedures and practices that they could never have witnessed or known about before.

With so many unmarked graves in the cemetery, not to mention Anne Marie Davee's remaining pieces, it's no wonder that the grounds are considered more haunted than the building itself. Many people believe that the tormented spirits of patients buried in unmarked graves still lurk, lost on the grounds.

These believers might be onto something, as just a few years ago more than 15 people called the police for what they described as a woman trespassing near the building, except that she was "glowing blue." By the time police arrived, the blue ghost was nowhere to be found, but the 15 witnesses remained adamant in what they saw. She was lurking near the entrance and appeared to be gardening, they all said.

Since the Metropolitan State Hospital became one of the World's Scariest Places, people began recording all sorts of disembodied whispers and unexplainable apparitions that are too clear to deny. But the crumbling and rotting hospital made for a sore sight for Boston and the surrounding towns, while the mysterious sightings on the grounds continued to frighten locals and attract ghost hunters.

By 2007, the hospital was completely demolished to make room for a complex of condos. It would seem that the eerie sounds, unexplained sightings, and desperate grabbing from the former residents were at an end—the stories and messages from the Hospital of Seven Teeth no longer heard.

But then again, the cemetery and every unidentified soul within it still linger to tell their tale.

PRIPYAT HOSPITAL

The MsCh-126 Medico-Sanitary, better known as Pripyat Hospital, once served the workers of the Chernobyl Nuclear Power Plant in Ukraine. Built in the 1970s with a 400-patient capacity, the state-of-the-art facility was the only hospital for Pripyat's 50,000 citizens.

No one really knew how important the hospital would become on April 26, 1986. Around midnight that day, Chernobyl engineers performed a routine test on Reactor Four. Then something went terribly wrong, causing the worst nuclear accident in history to date.

The nuclear fallout from the Chernobyl disaster was four times worse than the Hiroshima bombing, though few realized it during the hours and days that followed the disaster. Without knowing the nature of the accident, firefighters responded, wearing protective suits while dousing the fire. Not long after, they were all rushed to Pripyat Hospital after being exposed to lethal doses of radiation. It was here that most of the 47 accident workers died.

No one knows exactly what happened that night in 1986: what went wrong, how the reactor shattered so suddenly. While it's easy to see how the long-abandoned town gives people the creeps today, accounts of paranormal activity surrounded the town before the disaster in question.

In the week leading up to the infamous explosion on April 26, many reported seeing the most unnatural bird-like creature in the sky. The black monster had a 20-foot wingspan, sometimes appearing like a headless man, other times with red, glaring eyes. The creature would later be named the Black Bird of Chernobyl.

People who spotted the creature around Pripyat were later tormented by horrific nightmares and received mysterious, threatening phone calls before the disaster. Then, in the immediate aftermath of the explosion, several emergency workers claimed to see the winged beast circling through the smoke of the fire.

Maybe the first responders who claimed to see the monster were losing their senses to the intense radiation poising. Or maybe the Black Bird of Chernobyl brought some kind of reckoning on the people of Pripyat, while delivering not-so-subtle warnings in the week leading up to it. No one can say for sure—the chilling creature hasn't been seen in the ghost town since.

Paranormal buffs can't help but draw a connection between the Black Bird of Chernobyl and the Mothman seen in Point Pleasant, West Virginia. Also described as a large, winged creature with red eyes, the Mothman was seen throughout Point Pleasant in the days leading up to the collapse of Silver Bridge on December 15, 1968. Witnesses also experienced terrifying nightmares and phone threats after encountering the creature.

The similarities are striking, and it's unlikely that Ukrainian power plant workers had heard of the Mothman legend. Was this winged creature delivering some kind of warning to Pripyat and Point Pleasant, towns that were worlds apart but both heading for disaster?

After the initial accident, the citizens of Pripyat were slowly evacuated over the next few days. Officials told them they could return shortly, so many left their possessions behind. In reality, they would never go back. Almost overnight, Pripyat had become an enormous ghost city, and has remained that way for 28 years.

The hospital, once considered so modern, now lies untouched—filled with dirty and broken furniture. Writing on the roof reads, *Health of the people – riches of the country*. But it turns out the hospital could do little to keep the people of Pripyat healthy. Outside of the 47 deaths from first response workers, the disaster at Chernobyl has had more long-term effects. Children who were living in Pripyat at the time have now reported more than 6,000 cases of thyroid cancer due to radiation poising—nine of them have died so far.

As radiation levels have reduced enough to make it safe for short visits to Pripyat, it's become popular for tourists and adventurers to visit the largest ghost town in the world. However, the hospital itself still has its dangers. In the basement, you can find all the suits worn by firefighters who responded first during the disaster. Even after 28 years, they still carry a lethal dose of radiation.

It's generally believed that the ghost town of Pripyat is surely haunted, and visitors to the hospital in particular often feel like they are being watched. People claim to see apparitions or shadows—spirits of the victims of the Chernobyl disaster, mostly the firefighters who were rushed to the hospital from Reactor Four.

Though it would seem that not quite all of them made it that far. A chilling account by Andrei Kharsukhov, a nuclear physicist who visited Chernobyl in 1997, suggests that some might still be trapped in the reactor. While taking some readings near the sarcophagus of the reactor, he heard the distinct sounds of someone screaming for help within the reactor core.

"I ran upstairs to tell someone, but they said that when I entered the reactor control room, I was the first person to open that door in three years, and the only way to get inside the old reactor is through the doors I came in through. If someone had gone inside the reactor when I was not looking, they would have tripped an alarm that goes off when the reactor door is opened mechanically."

Kharsukhov shrugged off the sounds and went back to work. But later that evening while his team was eating dinner outside the reactor, a flood light suddenly turned on in the same room he had heard the cries for help. They stared in awe, wondering how anyone could be inside. Just as they decided that it must be a power surge, the light vanished.

Ghost hunters have since inspected Reactor Four, and to their shock, found a human figure on their thermal imaging camera inside of the reactor. During the chaos of that fateful day in April, rushing the poisoned firefighters to Pripyat Hospital had been a futile effort. Though it would seem that some of the men suffered an even worse fate—locked inside the infamous Reactor Four, where they remain to this day.

KUHN MEMORIAL STATE HOSPITAL

In 1832, smallpox outbreak left the community of Vicksburg, Mississippi in desperate need of help. Not long after, a small hospital was born, located between what is now downtown Vicksburg and the Vicksburg National Military Park.

At the time it was built, no one had any idea what tragedies and horror would plague the hospital throughout its long history. Despite its role as a place of healing, dark events have followed Kuhn Memorial State Hospital like the plague.

The modest hospital would go on to serve wounded during the Civil War, until the state took over operations in 1971, renaming it the State Charity Hospital at Vicksburg. Tragedy struck in 1878, as Yellow Fever wreaked havoc on the patients and staff. Sixteen doctors and six Catholic Sisters of Mercy lost their lives to the illness, while the number of patients who died remains unknown. But the hospital persevered, hosting the University of Mississippi's first medical school in 1910, and opening a wing to house Confederate veterans.

Then in 1918 a mysterious fire—still unexplained to this day—destroyed most of the annex. But the hospital rebuilt again, continuing to serve the sick and wounded of Vicksburg.

In 1954, it received its first stroke of real luck when an elderly man named Lee Kuhn passed away and left his $400,000 estate to the hospital. The money was used for further expansion, and the hospital was renamed Kuhn Memorial State Hospital, the name it carries to this day.

The hospital went on to serve all sorts of patients and people. The fourth floor became a minimum-security prison—inmates were required to perform menial tasks for the staff, such as clerking and cleaning. The Confederate Veterans Annex was specialized for patients with mental disabilities while The Pest House contained patients with infectious diseases. For once, the hospital thrived. But despite its utility to the community, it was closed in 1989 due to political and funding issues.

For more than two decades, Kuhn Memorial State Hospital lay empty—useless. The buildings crumbled and rusted, the interior molded. And like any empty building with easy access points, it attracted the attention of curiosity seekers and paranormal researchers.

America was a volatile place during the early years of the hospital's operation. A combination of war and primitive medical services ensured that many lost their lives at Kuhn. Ghost hunters searched for any lost souls that may have lingered and were often surprised with how easily they were found.

Though when two ghost hunters entered the old hospital in June 2015, they discovered something even more shocking than the spirits and apparitions they were searching for. In the building, they stumbled upon the body of Sharon Wilson, a 69-year-old woman who had only been reported missing only 12 hours before. They called the police, who found the death to be a homicide—Wilson had been murdered in the hospital shortly before the ghost hunters started their excursion. Two men were arrested quickly when they were discovered driving Wilson's car. No one knows exactly what happened to Wilson or why—the case is pending today.

What started out as spooky fun and games for paranormal researchers in an old building with a dark history became even more tragic. A roof of the front building started to collapse, prompting the state to talk seriously about demolishing the dilapidated complex. News reports from July 2015 say that on August 3, the historic hospital will be gone for good.

David Childers, co-founder of the Mississippi Paranormal Research Institute, who conducted several ghost hunts in the hospital, agreed with the decision to demolish the building. "There are open elevator shafts, black mold, asbestos, and debris, and people ought to stay away from that place," he told The Clarion Ledger. "Some spirits just need to be left alone."

THE OLD MENTAL HOSPITAL

Hong Kong is often viewed as one of the most modern cities in the world, full of new buildings with innovative designs. That's one of the reasons that a Victorian-style structure named The Old Mental Hospital is bound to get some strange looks from passers-by—found right in the middle of the city.

But if you dig just a little deeper into the past of the historic building, you'll find a lot of other—more *sinister*—reasons why The Old Mental Hospital stands out from the rest.

The original building was built in 1892 in the Sai Ying Pun area of Hong Kong. At nine stories tall, it first served as housing for the European nursing staff of the close-by Civil Hospital until the World War II. But like most wartime facilities that were established with the best intentions, the hospital was later repurposed for a much darker task.

According to urban legend, the Japanese used the hospital as a makeshift prison and execution hall during their occupation of Hong Kong. This may well have been true, as the Japanese commonly repurposed war hospitals to house anyone on the wrong side—or anyone they suspected of anti-Japanese sentiment—during the time. Rumor has it that many heads rolled to the floor in this house of healing, but only after a slew of torturous interrogation tactics.

After the war was over, the Old Mental Hospital was again repurposed into a mental institution, which is where it gets the modern rendition of its name. In 1947, the hospital was the only of its type in Hong Kong, which is unsettling considering that the city was home to half a million people at the time. Once Hong Kong got a better handle on providing mental health facilities, the hospital was then diminished to a day treatment center for psychiatric out-patients. That it remained from 1961-1971. The intention was to reopen the building for some new purpose after that, but two devastating fires, believed to be started by trespassers, made the building uninhabitable.

For twenty years after shutting down, the building remained unoccupied. Its historical architecture and expansive dark halls drew the attention of anyone who saw it, especially the local teenagers and drug addicts who visited the nearby methadone clinic.

As the building fell further and further into disrepair, people started reporting strange happenings—unwelcome reminders of the horrors of the war. The locals started calling it the Haunted House in High Street, named after the road it was built on, inadvertently choosing the perfect name for a ghost story.

Most of the ghost sightings you hear about in old, dilapidated buildings consist of disembodied whispers, distorted apparitions, and other unexplainable occurrences—often no one can say for sure whether they really saw something or not.

That was never the case at the Old Mental Hospital.

People have reported time and again seeing the clear figure of a mysterious, devil-like man dressed in traditional Chinese clothing. He commonly lurked on the second floor, and could have been confused for a local man hoping to scare people with a creepy costume, that is until he would summarily burst into flames shortly after being spotted—etching his image even further into the minds of unwanted visitors.

Still others have had the fright of their lives witnessing headless poltergeists running through the hallways in the dead of night. Could these be the troubled spirits of those tortured and executed dissidents during World War II? Many wonder.

After far too many break-ins and unending reports of ghostly encounters had started giving the neighborhood a bad name, the Old Mental Hospital was gutted and redeveloped as the Sai Ying Community Complex in

2001. Now, only the Victorian facade remains of what was once a dark and mysterious testament to the history of World War II.

That said, the shadows the sinister lighting cast over the high stone arches and empty verandahs still make it look incredibly haunted. According to Haider Kikabhoy, co-founder of Walk In Hong Kong, people who drive by the building still claim to hear ghostly voices, chilling screams, and visions of spirits, despite the building's current role as a community complex.

It would seem that gutting Old Mental was not enough to quell the cries and tantrums of the building's troubled spirits. Hong Kong recently classified the Old Mental Hospital as a Grade One Historic Building, so the complex, and all of its residents, are here to stay.

TRANS-ALLEGHENY LUNATIC ASYLUM

The town of Weston, West Virginia began construction on an insane asylum in 1858. The project, powered by prison labor, was an unprecedented undertaking, and took a long time—construction had to halt for the Civil War and resumed again in 1862. The hospital was built on 666 acres of land, as it was common knowledge at the time that pollutants of the cities were a main cause of insanity. Fresh air and open spaces would be the most advanced treatment offered to the mentally ill.

The goal for the Trans-Allegheny Lunatic Asylum was self-sufficiency, complete with a farm, dairy, waterworks, and cemetery. The second largest hand-cut stone building in the world (the Kremlin was larger), the hospital opened its doors officially in 1864. Per necessity, a separate section for African Americans was completed in 1873.

Despite such expansive grounds, Trans-Allegheny was designed to hold only 250 people. But that soon changed. By 1880 it held 717 patients; by 1938 it was up to 1,661 patients; there were more than 1,800 patients in 1949; patient population peaked at 2,400 in 1950.

According to a 1938 report by medical organizations, the hospital was home to "epileptics, alcoholics, drug addicts and non-educable mental defectives." Maybe they forgot to mention, or maybe it was in later years, that the hospital also housed children with Down's syndrome and diabetes, disabled veterans with nowhere else to go, people with syphilis before the advent of penicillin, and one couple with AIDS, who had their own personal apartment.

As it turns out, fresh air and distance from the hustle and bustle of the cities were likely the kindest treatments offered at the hospital. Frontal lobotomies and electro-shock therapy were commonly provided for the most difficult patients—helping them to calm down or at least instilling enough fear in them that they would comply.

Like many giant institutions at the time, overcrowding started to take its toll very early on. The Charleston Gazette wrote a series of exposés about the hospital in 1949 describing poor sanitation and the lack of supplies, furniture, lighting, and heating.

By the '70s and '80s, things managed to get even worse, despite a relative decrease in patient population. Reports of patients killing other patients passed without investigation, and female nurses and staff were often assaulted. One nurse went missing, only to be found dead at the bottom of an unused staircase nearly two months later. Doctors and staff started pulling out all the stops after that—patients who could not be controlled were now locked in cages.

It's pretty clear that no one will ever know the full extent of patient mistreatment during Trans-Allegheny's long history. Records from the hospital are amazingly incomplete—many patients who checked in never seemed to check out. In the hospital's private cemetery, headstones are missing. Others are just numbered bricks, leaving no clues about their occupants.

Hundreds are said to have died in the hospital, though, with such shoddy record-keeping, some think there could have been thousands. According to Andrea Lamb, a tour guide at the now derelict facility, families were often discouraged from contacting their loved ones who were committed to the hospital. "They were told, if they ever got a letter from them, to never even open it."

Years of newspaper reports tell of Weston residents complaining about hearing patient screams from outside the 666-acre premises. City officials finally decided it was time to build a new psychiatric facility in the late '80s, and made plans to turn Trans-Allegheny into a small prison.

In the end, the hospital closed in 1994 because of concerns about patient treatment, never to open again. Unfortunately, many of the patients who had spent most of their lives at Trans-Allegheny were moved to other facilities, only to suffer worse mental illness or to die mysteriously shortly after.

Despite being made a National Historic Landmark while still in operation, attempts to repurpose the building as a Civil War Museum were short-lived because of fire code violations. The mental asylum sat more or less empty for ten years, until the state auctioned it off to Joe Jordan, a private entrepreneur, in 2007.

After millions of dollars of renovations and asbestos removal, Jordan and his family repurposed the building for concerts, events—and haunted hospital tours. Today they offer paranormal tours six days a week, an increasingly popular attraction since the building was featured on several ghost hunting shows.

While many owners of old buildings repurposed as haunted houses have to make some effort to promote the idea that the building is haunted, Trans-Allegheny's dark history does it all by itself. Rebecca Jordan Gleason, the building manager, said, "I don't want to believe in ghosts or the supernatural, but I've seen things here that are hard to explain by any other way."

Most visitors never fail to experience some strange occurrence they can't explain—battery drainage, cold spots, voices, strange figures on heat-seeking cameras. Many report hearing the sound of gurneys being pushed down the long hallways, and screams coming from the electro-shock area. Others insist they saw full body apparitions of patients.

Some ghosts still living in the hospital appear light-hearted—giggling and laughing throughout the building. Others offer clear and ominous warnings to get out. Visitors to the hospital sometimes feel ill after departing, overcome with the shakes or a light-headed feeling.

The majority of ghost sightings throughout the hospital appear to be unique, which isn't surprising, considering the vast number of people who lived, suffered, and died at Trans-Allegheny. There is, however, one boy in particular who is seen over and over again, standing immobile in the corner of one room.

Grant Wilson of The Atlantic Paranormal Society claimed to see this boy as well, but got more of a show than others. He said the apparition put his hands over its head and looked like he was "being sucked out of the room." One other ghost, affectionately named Jacob, looks like a soldier and is often seen wandering around the Civil War wing.

While freaky things regularly occur throughout the old hospital, everyone agrees that the fourth floor is the most haunted. Strange sounds, banging, voices, and whispered conversations can be heard on the usually empty floor. Ghosts up there like to keep visitors on their toes. Once, Gleason witnessed 40 open doors on the fourth-floor hallway slam at once. "One would be pretty scary," Gleason said. "Forty at once was terrifying."

BEELITZ-HEILSTÄTTEN

Many Germans refer to the crumbling remains of Beelitz-Heilstätten as Berlin's biggest secret, hiding in plain sight. Built in 1898 in Southwest Berlin near Potsdam, the expansive hospital complex has a long history, standing witness to the fighting and sorrow of both world wars.

In the beginning, it was a simple sanatorium, built to house struggling tuberculosis patients as they fought their losing battle with a modest 600 beds. Expansion projects allowed Beelitz-Heilstätten to grow and care for the general sick of Berlin.

That was until August 3, 1914, when all the patients were evicted, and the hospital was taken over by the Red Cross. World War I was breaking out, and the German Imperial Army needed every bed.

The times were arduous, and casualties were high—the hospital treated 12,586 patients during the war. Among them was a young man named Adolf Hitler. Then a largely unknown army corporal, Hitler came to Beelitz-Heilstätten in October 1916. He spent two months in the hospital recovering from a leg wound sustained during British shelling at the Battle of Somme. No one knew he would walk out of the complex, going on to do bigger and more terrible things.

In 1920, the hospital was given a brief opportunity to go back to fighting the good fight: treating the general public. But soon enough it was time for World War II, and again the hospital was commandeered for military use. That made it a target, as several bomb attacks on the hospital were testament to. With much relief, the Nazis were defeated in 1945, and Germany was divided in two. Though that meant no reprieve for Beelitz-Heilstätten—the USSR took control of the complex and turned it into a Soviet military hospital.

As an important and useful structure amid the violence and uncertainties of two global wars, it's no surprise that Hitler wasn't the only infamous leader to grace Beelitz-Heilstätten with his presence.

On October 3, 1990, Germany was reunified as one country. Two months later, Erich Honecker, the disposed leader of the German Democratic Republic, was admitted to Beelitz-Heilstätten with liver cancer. Despite the seriousness of his illness, he only stayed for three months, since Germany had plans to hold him responsible for the deaths of 192 East German citizens who tried to flee the country over the Berlin Wall. Honecker ended up fleeing himself, towards Moscow and away from the wrath of justice.

Even as Soviet control of the country crumbled, the government wasn't in a hurry to pack up and move from Beelitz-Heilstätten. As the USSR maintained a tense grip on the hospital, a serial killer named The Beast of Beelitz, so named because most of his murders happened right by the hospital, was on the loose.

Between 1989-1991, The Beast of Beelitz, also known as Wolfgang Schmidt, murdered five women and one baby, and attacked several others. As a former police employee, he knew how to cover his steps and stumped the local police. Two of his victims were the wife and son of a doctor working at Beelitz. He killed the three-month-old baby boy by smashing his body into a tree stump. Then he gagged the mother with her bra, strangling her. After, he had sex with the body.

Schmidt gained another nickname, Rosa Riese, German for "pink giant." He was a very tall man and had a fetish for pink women's underwear, sometimes leaving a pair at his crime scene. He sexually assaulted almost all his victims. Finally, Schmidt was apprehended, not by the incompetent police, but by a couple of joggers who found him masturbating in a forest, wearing women's clothing.

If rejection by the country they once ruled wasn't enough to encourage the Soviets to abandon Beelitz-Heilstätten, maybe the threat of a local serial killer was. They finally abandoned the hospital in 1995, ending for good the hospital's century of intermittent military acquisition.

After that, attempts to completely privatize the complex were unsuccessful, and today only small parts of the 60-building hospital complex is used, serving as a neurological rehab center and a center for Parkinson's care and research. All the rest, including the surgery, psychiatric ward, and rifle range, were abandoned completely in 2000.

Since then, most of the abandoned complex has begun to decay, becoming an eerie testament to a hospital that saw so much difficult history. The derelict buildings are now covered in overgrowth, filled with rusty beds and vacant corridors smattered with graffiti. Some attempts have been made to restore the many buildings, but funds are seriously lacking.

As such a central piece of German history, the hospital is bound to attract people interested in taking a peek into the past. It's just as likely to attract mischief-makers and the homeless.

What's more surprising is the role it played as the scene of a sex game turned horribly wrong. In 2008, a young model named Anja met with fetish photographer Michael K. at Beelitz-Heilstätten for some sadomasochistic role-playing. Michael then lured her to an abandoned apartment on the edge of the complex, beat her on the head with a frying pan, strangled her to death, and had sex with her body. Another horrific murder-rape, reminiscent of The Beast of Beelitz.

According to Anja's agent, the level of realism in this role-play was not what her client had in mind. The apartment where she was brutally murdered was the former gatehouse of the complex, and remains available for rent today.

Today, the expansive grounds and numerous buildings at Beelitz-Heilstätten are surprisingly unsecured. Sure, things are locked up, but it's easy to find a way in to take eerie photos or get into some mischief.

With the hospital's extensive and dark history, it has become a mecca for neo-Nazis and Satanic worshippers, along with amateur ghost hunters, whose catalog of videos of ghostly encounters—too realistic to deny—grows year by year.

Between Beelitz-Heilstätten's role caring for terminally ill TB patients, its use in two world wars—including the treatment of two brutal dictators—and involvement in the exploits of two demented modern murderers, spiritual unrest on the grounds is a given.

Trespassers continue to loot, stirring up dust and old history, which only further disturbs the paranormal entities that reside restlessly there. But as a Grade II Historic Building, Beelitz-Heilstätten isn't going anywhere, other than slowly rotting away, a visual reminder of a dark and evil past.

WOLFE MANOR

Wolfe Manor was never your typical sanitarium and convalescent home. It was actually built as a large private home for Italian immigrant Tony Andriotti in Clovis, California in 1922. He ultimately couldn't afford the mansion and lost it.

The building didn't become a home to treat the terminally ill until 1935, when it was renamed Clovis Avenue Sanitarium. The 8000-square-foot mansion could only hold 100-150 patients at a time, but lax regulations and even weaker enforcement allowed the owners to house many more than was safe.

Clovis Avenue Sanitarium was always so crowded that patients were regularly forced to sleep in the halls. According to historians, there were often 20 patients assigned to one nurse.

The sanitarium sank further and further into a state of chaos over the years. People would visit only to find disturbing scenes of patients laying naked in the hallways or finding them tied to their bed or a toilet.

Staff were completely overwhelmed, and discussion of suicide and murder permeated the mansion and its patients. Possibly in an attempt to quell dangerous overcrowding and lack of staff control, a hospital wing for mental disorders was added on in 1954.

That did little to stem the alarmingly high death rate at Clovis Avenue. As such a small facility, it's astounding that thousands died there during its operation. With no morgue, and every available corner of the manor occupied by patient beds and supplies, the storing of the deceased became a problem. It was commonly known by locals, and confirmed by historians, that dead bodies would pile up in the basement, sometimes stacked eight high before someone came to pick them up.

As national health standards began to improve, it became clear that Clovis Avenue Sanitarium would never be a suitable facility. In 1992, it finally shut down, leaving behind a cringe-worthy history of overcrowding and mistreatment.

And so the Andriotti Mansion lay quiet, until local entrepreneur Todd Wolfe bought the building in 1997 and renamed it, Wolfe Manor. Wolfe saw the property for what it was—a spooky testament to a chilling history, so he turned it into a haunted attraction called, *Scream If You Can*. Running a successful haunted attraction, Wolfe hired staff to dress in scary costumes and frighten visitors.

What the workers never realized was how frightened they would become themselves.

"Things started happening, but I didn't want to tell anybody. One time, I felt a breath of air on my neck and another I was touched on my lower back," said Wolfe.

The owner was also bombarded by complaints of unexplainable occurrences from his staff. One claimed to have been pulled backwards into a room, only to find the room empty—no one was there. It became a common occurrence for workers to quit without notice—claiming that too many creepy things kept happening to them.

The strangest story of an unexplainable occurrence came directly from the Clovis Police Department. They received, and responded to, numerous 911 calls and alarms from the mansion, only to find no one there and no apparent emergency.

The strangest part is that as a haunted house attraction, the building had not been equipped with an alarm system or a telephone. Who in the world was calling? More importantly, how were the calls going through?

Visitors to the Halloween attraction were obviously in the mood for some haunted thrills, but many got a lot more than they bargained for. Guests regularly reported feeling chills and being shoved by someone lurking, unseen. The worst affected found themselves inexplicably sick to their stomachs and light headed.

The manor also seemed to come with a cast of characters that Wolfe never hired to scare anyone, seen so often that they were given names by the guests. Mary, the figure of an elderly woman, can be found lurking the halls. Many others see Emily, a young girl who doesn't belong. A few others have seen a figure that is difficult to describe. They called him "man baby," and left in a hurry.

The unwanted disturbances of staff and guests became enough that Wolfe, an overall skeptic, enlisted the help of a psychic to inspect the home. Once they offered their opinion that the mansion was a hotbed of paranormal activity, ghost hunters came far and wide to see for themselves. What followed was hundreds of EVP recordings, photographs, and videos of unexplained figures and apparitions and disembodied voices that make your hair stand on end.

Wolfe Manor continued as a successful haunted house for some time, where staged attractions and hired characters became secondary to the frightening occurrences the mansion produced itself. But Scream If You Can came to a halt in 2004 because of noise complaints.

Wolfe kept the building, but it lay vacant and quiet—for the most part. Its popularity as one of the most haunted spots in the western US attracted many vandals, interested in the building's frightening history.

Then in 2011, the city of Clovis decided the building was frightening in more than one way. Wolfe Manor's state of disrepair, including cracking, dry rot, and broken windows had made it unsafe to occupy.

It had also been labeled a hot spot; police were constantly putting out unexplained fires on the property—reporting 96 police calls regarding the mansion since 2008. It was never explained why the fires kept occurring; the groundskeeper said that break-ins had reduced considerably over the years.

Could it be the work of trapped spirits, hoping for a way out of the hospital where so many people suffered and lost their lives? If that's the case, the city of Clovis heeded their message and demolished Wolfe Manor in November 2014.

For those who believe, the hope is that with the teenage revelers gone and the building demolished, the overcrowded spirits of Clovis Avenue Sanitarium can finally rest—freed from the beds they were once chained to and the basement where their bodies laid forgotten.

WHITTINGHAM MENTAL HOSPITAL

During the late 19th century, three mental asylums in Lancaster, England were deemed completely full, prompting the region to build Whittingham Mental Hospital, which opened its doors in 1873.

In a time when mass institutionalization was considered the best practice to handle the mentally ill, the hospital was viewed with pride in the area. A church, some farms, a railway, a telephone exchange, a post office, reservoirs, and a brewery all belonged to Whittingham. Don't forget the orchestra, brass band, ballroom, and butcher, too.

It opened with a capacity of 1100 patients but soon several annexes were added, including a sanatorium for people with infectious diseases. With a total capacity of 3,533 people, Whittingham became the largest mental hospital in Britain.

Where did all these "lunatics" come from, you ask? The simple answer: most of the patients weren't certifiably crazy in the first place. It would seem that extreme poverty had a way of making people act out in ways that weren't considered normal. It was these "pauper lunatics" that Whittingham was specifically designed for.

It became the asylum where the government sent patients that had no one to pay for their care. Historians have become skeptical about just how insane these pauper lunatics actually were. Most intake records were frustratingly vague, leaving no notes other than "insane seaman" or "acute mania." The records go on to show that these patients lived the rest of their lives at Whittingham.

Despite such a low rate of patient recovery at Whittingham, the hospital was considered a pioneer in electroencephalograms (EEGs), by experimenting with the treatment on patients, no less. The technology was supposedly an incredible therapy tool for many—for others, it was the opposite.

Twentieth-century England was a very volatile place, and Whittingham witnessed some of the worst of the history. During the First World War, many of the hospital's doctors were drafted, while the nurses volunteered. The largest mental hospital in Britain became desperately strapped for staff.

Still, in 1918 the New West Annexe of the hospital was repurposed to treat war casualties for one gruesome year.

People who died there were buried in the private cemetery. Two other wards were repurposed during World War II, from 1939 to 1946, to treat military and civilian casualties alike.

After the great wars were done, one would hope that the strain on patient care at Whittingham would subside. Unfortunately, the worst was yet to come.

In the 1960s, some workers witnessed what they described as serious cruelty and ill-treatment towards patients, as well as fraud in the hospital administration. In 1967, the Student Nurses Association filed a complaint, but they didn't get far. The head male nurse at Whittingham gathered the students, threatened them with libel and slander, and told them to "put up or shut up."

The students were silenced for a time, but once more people witnessed the mistreatment, the Hospital Management Committee was forced to investigate. What they discovered about the treatment of patients at Whittingham was disturbing.

In Ward 3, a male ward, patients were subjected to a "wet towel treatment." For patients who just couldn't behave themselves, nurses would take a wet towel or sheet, and hang it around the patient's neck until they calmed down and fell unconscious.

In Ward S2, two other nurses would put methylated spirits into the slippers and pockets of patients' bathrobes and set them on fire as some form of cruel punishment.

The worst treatment of all was for the women of Ward 16. Here, patients were routinely locked outside in all sorts of weather, or in washrooms and cupboards, to discourage bad behavior. Patient ailments were left untreated, and at times they were only fed bread and jam, served as slops. Some nurses enforced fluid restrictions during and after meals, others tied unruly patients to their beds wearing only vests. One woman was dragged about by the hair. Disturbingly, this hellish ward was under the direction of the same Catholic sister for 47 years.

It seemed that in Whittingham's long years in operation, the hospital had descended into anarchy. Wards were infested with cockroaches, ants, and even mice, crawling over patients who were unable to leave their beds.

Most of the hospital hovered at unstable living temperatures—46 degrees F or less. The hospital staff developed a culture of petty theft between wards. In the upper ranks, serious fraud and embezzlement took money right out of patients' pockets. Money earmarked for patient care went instead to build expensive condos for hospital administrators.

Once the atrocities at Whittingham came to light, the head nurse and Head Matron took early retirement. Two other nurses were convicted of theft while another nurse was imprisoned for manslaughter after an elderly patient he assaulted died.

All we can say for sure about patient mistreatment at Whittingham is what student nurses and patients were able to prove in court. But everyone knew it was nothing close to the full extent of suffering at Whittingham in its many years of operation.

After the inquiry, the hospital limped on under the watchful eyes of administrators, carrying a dark label and countless stories of cruelty. Despite efforts to redevelop the hospital into something new, creepy relics from its unsettling past lingered on to tell the tale the patients couldn't.

Lawrence Butterfield was a worker at Whittingham in the mid-eighties and recalls spooky occurrences at the hospital after its darkest years were over. Working the night shift, Butterfield had a prime opportunity to become jolted by things that go bump in the night.

Not much seemed to faze him, though, until one night when he was visiting with another staff nurse after all the patents had gone to sleep. Suddenly his colleague became very quiet, and her face contorted into a look of confusion and fear as she watched Butterfield. When he asked her what was wrong, she said that she had seen what she could only describe as a monkey shape, hovering just above his shoulder. It had disappeared before Bufferfield could notice, but both nurses were left unsettled.

All the staff at Whittingham had an aversion to one corridor of the hospital in particular. According to

Butterfield, it was "notorious...for weird occurrences." Filled with windows that looked into older wards packed with old beds and furniture from Whittingham's dark past, unexplained sounds and mysterious power shortages were only some of the strange experiences workers and patients had in this one hallway. But it served as a shortcut around the hospital, so they used it regularly. Once, Butterfield had the overwhelming feeling that someone was watching him in the corridor, frightening him enough to scurry his way to safety.

Between a bad reputation, decreased patient load, and increasingly unsettling atmosphere at Whittingham, the hospital closed down in 1995. As you might expect, the abandoned hospital has developed a new reputation for unexplained phenomena. The empty halls seem to have minds of their own—voices can be heard behind locked doors, and strange sightings have left many midnight thrill-seekers scrambling to leave the building.

With its history of locking up the poor, experimental treatments, suffering the strains of two wars, and the rampant patient mistreatment that followed, the hospital seemed to dabble in all the worst parts of the history of mass institutionalization. It's no wonder the hospital's many wards send chills down any visitor's spine.

Some might say that the tortured patients of Whittingham never received real justice for the behavior of the staff, and seek revenge on whoever might still linger in the buildings. But aside from the occasional trespasser, life and suffering at Whittingham are over, and the buildings continue to rot.

SLEEP WELL

So this is the end of a unique compilation of hauntings from abandoned hospitals around the world. I hope you learned more about the long and sometimes brutal histories of these institutions. But more importantly, I hope you were scared silly!

While some of these old and haunted buildings have been demolished—or will be by the time this book is published—just as many others are protected for their historical value, and are here to stay. Though they'll never again see the long days of treating and mistreating patients—and of understaffing, epidemic diseases, and wartime appropriation.

But whether it be faint whispers in the hallway, unexplained bouncing balls, slamming doors, groping of unseen hands, or the screams of a decapitated poltergeist—the ghosts of these abandoned hospitals will continue to tell their story. And as we learn more about these disturbing occurrences through first-hand accounts, eerie photos, disturbing videos, and EVP's, more and more people will begin to listen.

While we now know much more about the difficult lives and suffering deaths many spirits experienced in these facilities, we still haven't answered the ultimate question about why these lost souls continue to send chills down our spines and haunt our dreams as well as these old hospitals.

What do they want?

DID YOU ENJOY *HAUNTED HOSPITALS AND MENTAL ASYLUMS?*

Again let me thank you for purchasing and reading this short collection of stories. There are a number of great books out there, so I really appreciate you choosing this one.

If you enjoyed the book, I'd like to ask for a small favor in return. If possible, I'd love for you to take a couple of minutes to leave a review for this book on Amazon. Your feedback will help me to make improvements to this book, as well as writing books on other topics that might be of interest to you!

OTHER BOOKS BY ZACHERY KNOWLES

Real Haunted Ouija Boards

Real Haunted Cemeteries and Graveyards

Real Demonic Possessions and Exorcisms

Real Haunted Woods and Forests

Real Police Ghost Stories

Real Haunted Castles and Fortresses

Real Haunted Hospitals and Mental Asylums

Real Hauntings at Sea

FREE GIFT REMINDER

Before you finish, I'd like to remind you one more time of the free eBook I'm offering to readers of my *True Ghost Stories* series.

To instantly download the PDF version of my book, *Real Black-Eyed Kids*, all you need to do is visit:

www.realhorror.net

Printed in Great Britain
by Amazon